Mission Possible

Mission Possible

If You Move; God Moves

Katie B. Newborn

KN Ministries
P.O. Box 1692 Mansfield, Texas 76063
www.knministries.us

Cover Design by: Khromatix Solutions

Dedication

To my Mother, who prayed for me, who loved me, who pushed me and assured me that "God Doesn't Make Any Mistakes". May she who is now apart of the great cloud of witnesses in heaven continue to see me run this race.

To my father, thank you for being the example of strength I have referenced for every challenge in my life. Your determination and never quitting shall forever be my guiding light.

Table of Contents

Introduction

This book is going to help you take the next step toward your purpose. You'll learn that each step makes your *Mission Possible*. To be challenged to live in the divine destiny you were created for.

Even when everything inside and around you screams failure, you'll be ensured that your purpose is real and world-changing. All you have to do is *move*. Start your great journey through small steps strategically maneuvered. Small steps that will grow to eradicate obstacles that stand between you and your Mission.

During the industrial revolution of Japan, a key business philosophy used to create a successful movement in innovation was, "Kaizen". A philosophy of all taking small steps of continuous improvement of practices and personal efficiency until the greater task is accomplished. Deliberate small efforts that keep you on course for success.

It's your turn to recreate your world. Activate your small steps toward your *Mission Possible*.

I'll be honest, the assigned mission, given me by the Lord, has seemed impossible to achieve. However, as I continued to surrender and take steps, God continues to make all things very much possible.

Calling all those who sense a purpose for their life and power greater than themselves. This one's for you.

Through real stories of my unpredictable life experiences, I hope to entertain, encourage, motivate, and inspire you. The kind that captures you from the inside out and forces you to move! Take action on your passions and intimidations.

I pray you acknowledge that whatever the purpose, assignment, or mission; you can accomplish it. With God, it is a *Mission Possible*.

Kaizen: *'A Good Change'*

During the 1980s, the quest for global competition brought forth the philosophy and implementation of the Kaizen concepts. The Japanese word kaizen simply means "change for better". The word in English is typically applied to measures for implementing continuous improvement, especially those with a "Japanese philosophy".

In business, kaizen refers to activities that continuously improve all functions and involve all employees from the CEO to the assembly line workers. It also applies to processes, such as purchasing and logistics that cross organizational boundaries into the supply chain. It has been applied in healthcare, psychotherapy, life-coaching, government, banking, and other industries. Kaizen was first practiced in Japanese businesses after the Second World War, influenced in part by American business and quality-management teachers, and most notably as part of The Toyota Way. It has since spread throughout the world and has been applied to environments outside of business and productivity.

Kaizen is a daily process, the purpose of which goes beyond simple productivity improvement. It is also a process that, when done correctly, humanizes the workplace, eliminates overly hard work (muri), and teaches people how to perform experiments on their work using the scientific method and how to learn to spot and eliminate waste in business processes. In all, the process suggests a humanized approach to workers and to increasing productivity. The idea is to nurture the company's people as much as it is to praise and encourage participation in kaizen activities. Successful implementation requires the participation of workers in the improvement. This concept has become so infused in the Japanese business culture that it has become second nature to the natives.

The Kaizen philosophy assumes that our way of life; whether working, social, or our home life, deserves to be constantly improved. This Japanese philosophy for process improvement has a name made up of two Japanese words, "Kai and Zen", meaning *to break apart and investigate or to improve upon the existing situation.* The objectives of Kaizen are teamwork, discipline, motivation, exposure, exchange and involvement. An astronomical idea of never being satisfied with what was already accomplished but, eager to strategize another solution. Improvement begins with the admission that every problem provides an opportunity for change.

The cycle of kaizen: "Plan → Do → Check → Act", also known as PDCA.

Overall, the kaizen principle embodies ideals and strategies that have proven to improve our way of thinking and life outcomes. Get ready to explore how this ancient principle matches with God's word in reference to how we should pursue our purpose and success in life.

Chapter 1

Mission Possible (All Things Are Possible)

Chapter 1
Mission Possible (All Things Are Possible)

With men this is impossible, but all things are possible with God.

Matthew 19:26 (NIV)

I can vividly remember several groggy days of sitting at my desk on a job that was no longer fulfilling. Rummaging through my life repository wondering how I ended up here. Sitting in my own emptiness, I was awakened with a desire to seek more. I started on a journey to find something to fill this emptiness. I signed up for a mission trip to travel to a new place for a new experience, with the mere expectation of a peaceful journey. My mindset was that this would allow me to escape the familiar and delve into a different world of opportunity. At that time, I didn't know how correct I was. After ten hours of riding in a crowded, fifteen-passenger van with oversized luggage taking up the back seat and varying sized individuals squeezed against one another; my mind was made up that I would not be on this journey, ever again! However, being in a van with no way out, kind of delayed taking that action for the moment. After arriving in country at our destination, the heat of August beamed down on us as we immediately began our outreach projects. We walked the paved streets offering rice and beans to those in need, praying for those who wanted prayer, and inviting everyone we met to come to the neighborhood church's night service. The presence of God was definitely with us. By the end of the evening, we were all exhausted from the heat, the long ride, and lack of sleep.

However, our day wasn't done, yet. That night service we invited everyone to was about to begin. We stumbled into the church sweaty, smelly, exhausted and despondent. We walked into an exuberant worship service already in progress. There was something happening in the atmosphere. The entire church was on their knees singing in worship. Music and electricity filled the air. We sat, glued to our seats, taking it all in and getting a much needed refreshing. Eventually, the

Pastor saw how obviously drained we were. He called us all to the altar and began praying for us, individually.

One by one, each released the weight of the burdens they were carrying. While I waited for the Pastor to pray for me, I was secretly negotiating with God. Strategizing a way out of this decision and promising that I would never, ever return here. "Am I where I should be; doing what I should be doing?", I inquired in my mind. I begged God, most of all, to get me back home. Back to my boring, unfulfilling life behind a desk.

This "trip" had challenged every fiber of my being. I didn't know what God wanted me to do but I was positive this could not be it.

Finally, it was my turn for prayer. The Pastor simply stated, "You are supposed to be here". Those few words changed the trajectory of my life. Immediately, my negotiating ended with complete surrender. Who else, but God could know what I was thinking. Without fully understanding, I began to focus all my efforts, both internal and external in my life, toward that declaration. "You are supposed to be here."

At this point in my life, I had never traveled outside of the country. Faith and belief aligned in me with the word spoken in private to me by God. "I'm going to send you to the Nations", he announced in a still quiet voice. At the time, my heart and soul weren't ready to receive what I'd just heard, even though I had experienced glimpses of this prophecy coming true. First, on my trip to Mexico and for some time following. It wasn't until one day, after returning from several mission trips around the world, I realized that I was living the word spoken to me.

It happened so suddenly. Like me at that time, you could be living in your purpose and not even know it. And because we don't know we're right where we're supposed to be, we use our energy complaining and begging God for something else. Something, we think, is better. These actions actually hinder us from reaping the fullness of the benefits of living out our purpose and residing in the will of

God. When I realized what my ungrateful attitude was risking, I quickly made the needed adjustments to my perspective and my actions.

If you are longing for a *Mission Possible* kind of experience in your life, the kind that blows your mind and changes your forever, I strongly encourage you to move with every opportunity while understanding that your gift of contribution to the world is invaluable. I believe, inspiration indicates that within you there is some pre destined gift in you to impact the world.

I pray that you will freely begin the process of finding your hidden treasures and opportunities and that they will expose you to the world in ways you couldn't dream of. Awakening within you a hope and desire that extends beyond you and engulfs the whole world.

Regardless of where you are in your life, you mustn't give up hope. You cannot expect or look for a quick transformation. The process of change happens over time. However, your opportunities and experiences will change and develop continuously. We are all changing and growing daily. However, there will be signs of growth throughout the cycle. Your focus should be on what is set before you. Your goals, mission, ministry, and the promises of God. Look for every opportunity to enhance, grow, increase, learn, change, and harmonize to balance your development.

There will always be obstacles, but

remember, everything you need to overcome

them is already inside you. Just tap into your

God-given gifts.

Chapter 2

Everybody Brings Something to The Table

Chapter 2

Everybody Brings Something to The Table

For those whom He foreknew (and loved and chose beforehand) (ref. Jeremiah 1:5), He also predestined to be conformed to the image of His Son (and ultimately share in His complete sanctification), so that He would be the first born (the most beloved and honored) among many believers.

Romans 8:29 (ABV)

Efficiently utilizing your experiences and gifts creates the maximum opportunity for your greatest works to show forth. You can become a catalyst to change in the world. What you are made of is unique, unlike anyone else. That means only you can make the difference you were meant to make. However, you are not alone. Each of us must carry the responsibility of being our brother's keeper. We must function knowing that we are fitly joined together.

Remember: What I do affects you, and what you do affects me.

Sharing hope in the world means, recognizing the relevancy of each individual and how we all coordinate an ensemble emphasizing the importance of each doing a part but subordinating personal prominence to the efficiency of the whole.

Because I was willing to surrender my expectations, I've had the opportunity to travel from nation to nation, sharing hope and love. Each destination taught me something

new about myself and my mission from God.
I remember seeing shoes flying off the back
of a truck because of the desperation to
receive a pair while in Africa providing
medical assistance and shoes. I experienced
the world under the sea in Belize, as we
administered hygiene items in the local
prison. Spending Christmas at the railroad
track and dump community in Mexico,
passing out blankets, bottled water, and
playing games with the children. Enduring the
longest walk of my life in the Dominican
Republic, while walking down a massive hill
into a hidden impoverished community,
located near a disease-infested river to bring
its residents purified water. Sharing words of
encouragement in the brothels of Cambodia

and the Dominican Republic to individuals entangled in human trafficking, and teddy bears in a Christmas tree in a home setup for the children rescued from trafficking. Finding myself walking in the purpose of my life, all the while questioning if this is even something that I could do. Discovering that the mission assigned to my life that was seeming, very much impossible for me to accomplish, has become a *Mission Possible*.

Tip from the

Author:

Motivation will

continuously assist in

your success. Along

your journey, look for

inspiration to continue

improvement and

movement!

———————

Even our salvation is not coincidental, but

planned by God. He, prior to our existence,

determined and set us aside for his purpose.

He already knows our end before our

beginning and has it all under his control.

Remember, there are some things God knows

about you that you may not know about

yourself. Seek him for the revealing of those

hidden treasures within you and move with

action on every gift. Treasure is excavated,

which means that it may emerge flawed. The

excavator may have to remove some dirt, debris, and rocks to reveal the gem's best features.

When your treasures are revealed, in God's timing, you will show forth his glory.

Chapter 3

Christmas at the Dumps in Mexico

Chapter 3
Christmas at the dumps in Mexico

But my God shall supply all your need according to his riches in glory by Christ Jesus.

Philippians 4:19 (King James Version)

One of my many mission outreaches into Mexico was to the trash dump community. Families built their homes from whatever they could find in the dump fields. The children would gather dirty old cardboard boxes, plastic, tin, sticks, and any other tangible items they deemed useful for constructing their make-shift home. Even with the risks of the dangers lurking underneath the trash heaps, this is the youth's' daily task. As our team drove vans into the area of the dump on uncharted roads, we observed the environment in which the children and their families lived every day.

This type of environment would distract any child from the joys of childhood, like playing. However, as the team drove up in our vans the children came running from every direction. Some without shoes, others with tattered clothing, shuffled hair, and dirty little faces. Looking into their eyes, you could still see bright glimmers of inspiration and hope. They had an internal light that shined externally everywhere they went.

Our team provided small household items, such as blankets, water, and toys for the children who don't usually get to experience Christmas. We sang songs, played games and offered an opportunity for prayer. Everyone was very receptive to receiving prayer. As we played with the children around the trash dump, you could notice some of the team members becoming very overwhelmed by the children's reality.

Tip from the Author:

Become a person who is willing to freely give. One of the beauties of this journey is meeting, helping, and connecting with others along the way. Open your heart to

be a blessing, used by

God. You give yourself

more opportunities to

experience and grow.

The enthusiasm and genuine appreciation the

children showed for their Christmas gifts,

changed each one of us. In fact, the entire

environment around the dump had

transformed with a fresh breeze of joy. I

found myself reminiscing on my Christmas

experiences as a child. These children seemed

to be elated about the basic items they

received. I, too, remember Christmas

revolving around the things we needed.

Anything extra was an unexpected treat.

Treats that I began to expect as the norm in my life as an adult.

That thought energized a humbling epiphany within me of how easily one can overlook the daily blessings in their very own life. I withdrew for a moment to thank God for the simple blessings I had been ignoring. I felt impressed to thank Him for always supplying my needs.

How often do you take a moment to assess where you are in life and what you have right now? After returning from my moment of self-reflection, I joined the celebration at the dump with wholehearted joy and thankfulness. I left Mexico with a filled heart and a determination to be grateful in every situation, and have applied it

continuously in my life.

Chapter 4

Shoes Flying In Africa

Chapter 4
Shoes Flying In Africa

*Blessed shalt thou be when thou comest in,
and blessed shalt thou be when thou goest
out.*

Deuteronomy 28:6 (KJV)

My first outreach mission was in

Kenya, Africa. I led a team of trained

missionaries. Our objectives were to set up

for medical camps and distribute shoes to the

visiting natives. We provided strategic

planning, setup, and support for three medical

camps. One location was in, what is called,

"the Bush". The second was in conjunction

with a hospital and the third, within what

would be considered a slum community. All

the logistics were planned ahead, but from experience, we all knew that we have to be fluid in preparation for the unexpected.

What I knew that others didn't know was that my unexpected had already happened. Just prior to leaving for the outreach, my mother had become extremely sick. The family was called home to address the issue she was facing. She had been taken to the hospital for a blood transfusion and the doctors were unable to determine why her blood levels had dropped so low. I traveled home to see her. While there, I talked to her about the upcoming outreach. She knew about each outreach I served on because she was my prayer warrior. She also got a unique gift from every location as a souvenir. She has always been the strongest woman I know so when I shared that I was thinking about not going, I wasn't surprised that she released me to go forth in the things that God was doing in my life.

"Don't worry about me, God is good. I'll be alright", she assured me.

Well, *she* was strong, but I wasn't so sure that I could handle anything happening to her while I was in Africa. I prayed and asked God to watch over my mother and my family as I went forth to do His will. However, I must admit it was always in the back of my mind. This mental battle made me physically and emotionally sensitive and caused a few secret and open moments of tears. To cope, I would replay her words over and over in my head, "God is good and I'll be alright." In addition, I had faith in my prayer request that God would keep her and my family. He did just that.

On my plane ride, I could hear in my spirit, you were born for such a time as this. After landing in Africa and seeing the surprising beauty of the country, I was overwhelmed with amazement. Those words, etched in my spirit on the plane, turned me into a sponge during the entire outreach. I spent every moment searching for what I was to learn from this experience, knowing that God had predetermined this for my life. The entire outreach was surreal in that I was standing in the promise of God.

He had previously revealed that he would send me to the nations. I still didn't fully understand, in that moment, that I am experiencing just what he said. I was standing among a nation of people and in a country for which I had no points of reference. I could never have imagined an experience like this! Each day I grew more humble with expectation in God and offered complete submission to His plan for my life.

The medical camp, conducted in the bush, was a convenience for many who could not make the long trip into the city because of their health, age, or resources. Our team was able to provide medical services to hundreds in need. Individuals from all around the area came for care. Medical services were provided for a variety of illnesses. The talented doctors we worked beside were able to provide medical care in the most rugged terrain with minimal technology. I could tell from their enthusiastic conversations that this experience was changing them, too. God was at work already, and this was just our first medical camp.

Later in the outreach, we were able to go back out to the Bush and spend time with the tribe members. They wanted to honor our mission team and show their appreciation for the services we provided. We were invited into their homes, built from cow dung, and shown how they conduct day to day activities. The dung was left outside an area of the camp until it completely fermented and dried and was able to be used. When ready, it was applied to the sides of their huts to provide structure and coverage from the elements. The huts were small in size but sufficient for the need of the family. It usually included a place for cooking, sleeping, and a small sitting area. There is no plumbing, electricity, or any modern amenities. The majority of their social activity occurs outside.

The women are responsible for gathering the water needed to cook, clean, and bath. Their efforts to gather the needed water could be an all-day task depending on the distance required to walk to the nearest water source.

Our team was part of a bigger effort to provide this tribe with a functional water well, which saved them time, gave young girls the opportunity of education, and increased the women's health by eradicating the number of labors and births on the long road to retrieve water.

The water well was located in a neutral location to allow access to multiple tribes and villages. This access, location, and abundance of water helped resolve feuds amongst the tribes.

The celebration included the preparation and cooking of a cow in an underground pit covered with tree branches. The smell of the cooking meat filled the air as the women on the team assisted the tribal women with the cultural preparation of a side dish of porridge. The men on the team were seated with the tribal elders and men in, what seemed to be, deep discussions.

As we gathered around the makeshift table, the men were served first from the roasted cow, and then the women received their meat. The taste was very different from what I was used to. It didn't taste cured and had no seasoning, at all. However, the custom is to receive and partake of what is in front of you, gratefully. The killing and serving of a cow was a huge gesture for the tribe because that is their primary sustenance. So, it would be very impolite to not show appreciation and gratitude.

But, after a few chews, the taste was more than many of us on the team could handle. We found modest and candid ways to get it out of our mouths without bringing attention to ourselves. I nonchalantly filled my pockets with half chewed cow. But, it smelled impeccable.

Soon, we came to the realization that we had stayed in the Bush too long when several of us, women, had to use the bathroom. Oops, spoiler alert, the "bathroom" is a hole in the ground. You know, as first-world women, we were immediately against the idea, but you've got to do what you've got to do. So one by one we lined up, provided coverage for each other and had our own individual experience with the Bush.

It was a long ride back to the city. The second outreach was conducted in partnership with a small local community hospital and their team of local doctors and nurses. Our team of doctors worked in unison with their staff and the non-medical personnel set up triage area, a pharmacy for nurses to dispense prescriptions written by the doctors during the medical outreach, staged an area for the disbursement of maze for those attending the medical camp and, offered prayer for those waiting in line for medical services.

This camp had thousands of individuals lined up for help and services. The people serviced at this camp suffered from all kinds of illnesses. Even the most minor illness had been exasperated to very serious symptoms.

The line to receive service from the local physicians started early, stayed all day, and remained even after our team left. One of the doctors that traveled with our team got to experience conducting a surgery with medical equipment that was out dated, compared to the top of the line equipment that he normally used. It had such an impact on him in that moment he couldn't stop talking about it. I'm convinced it changed his life. Everything about him reflected new levels of confidence and assurance.

We spent hours praying for the needs of those in line. Their receptivity and agreement created a charged atmosphere of hope and expectation that was felt by everyone. Our prayers were empowered with hope and faith. You could practically see the weight of burden lifting from them, even while they waited in line. You could feel their faith. With every ounce of their being they knew that if they could just see the doctors, they would get better. There was healing and rejoicing all around. Praise be to God!

Our team did not want to leave, but for security reasons, we had to leave the neighborhood before nightfall. The bus ride back to the hotel was overflowing with testimonies and joyous praises to heaven. Everyone had great expectation and praise reports to share.

The third medical camp was in an area considered the Slums. Slums, in Africa, are huge communities with a large population of people closely located in a small space of land. The community we served had thousands of people living in makeshift housing. There is no electric, no plumbing, and the community had an open sewage system. We coordinated with the local nurse assigned to the community clinic to assist with implementation of the medical camp. Along with the medical camp, we planned to wash feet and distribute new socks and tennis shoes. This location, because of its reputation, required additional support by security personnel. We would be taking all of our supplies into the community and needed to ensure safe transport.

The day we arrived for the medical camp, we found that the community's "clinic" was an extremely small, one room shack unable to house our supplies. Also, that there was one way into the community and one way out. But we remembered that we had to be fluid. After a quick assessment, it was determined that the camp would be set up near the clinic, located at the front entrance of the community. The security team believed that this would allow us to maintain the best control of our environment. Based on their expert opinion, we set up the medical camp in front of the clinic, which included the main highway running in front of it with a bus stop.

We started by serving the women and children first and set up a perimeter for the foot washing stations. In the foot washing stations, we had our supply of shoes and socks. At the beginning, we could tell it was going to be a challenge providing the level of service necessary. The shoes and socks had become somewhat of a distraction. We directed the individuals to line up for the clinic services first, and afterward, they could enter the foot washing station. Well, the order lasted a short period of time.

As the team washed feet, we prayed for the individuals, gave them new socks and shoes, and witnessed transformation take place. The children's eyes lit up like shining stars and the women were humbled to weeping. After a number of individuals received their new socks and shoes, the word began to spread among the community. Before we knew it, a huge crowd had gathered around us. We soon found ourselves engulfed by hundreds of people who were desperate to receive new socks and shoes. We were determined to try and serve as many people as possible. One special story was an elderly man, in his eighties, who, we soon learned, had never owned a pair of shoes in his life. The receipt of the new socks and shoes brought him to joyous tears. He could not believe that his lifelong dream had come true, in that very moment.

After a while, we realized that the press of the crowd had grown to a level of concern for the security team. It was decided that we should shut down the camp and began the process of removing our team. The strategy was to relieve the one member at a time so that closing down would not be obvious or frustrate the people. One by one, team members gathered a few supplies and returned to the buses.

After all of the women on the team had loaded the buses, the men and security team loaded the truck with the few remaining shoes and we all left the community. However, we had not anticipated the level of desperation for the shoes. As we traveled from the community, some of the men from the community began to jump onto the back of the truck and throw shoes from the back. We could see the shoes flying off the truck as we followed the van.

Our security team was eventually able to halt the men and stop the shoes from flying. The men's tenacity was not overlooked.

Arrangements were made for the community leaders to disburse the remaining shoes another day. Those who lived in the slum community and others, who desperately needed the shoes, were blessed. Watching those shoes fly affirmed that the smallest need supplied is *still* a huge blessing.

Chapter 5

Another World Under The Sea... In Belize

Chapter 5
Another World Under The Sea... In Belize

And we know that all things work together for good to them that love God, to them who are called according to his purpose.

Romans 8:28 (KJV)

Imagine me, dawning of a gas mask, during a high-combat training session in the United States Army. While on active duty in the United States Army, I experienced one of my most agonizing moments during a routine tear gas training. My platoon was marched to a remote location. As we approached our destination, we could see these tents set up. The closer we approached to the camp we encountered individuals running out of the tents and vomiting violently.

Outside, there were areas set up to teach individuals how to put on and wear their gas mask properly. We were required to enter the tent and endure the choking gas for a few seconds before donning the gas mask as we were trained. (Put the mask on our face and remove the air by sucking until the mask is tightly sealed) The intense burning of the gas made it almost impossible to focus and concentrate on getting the mask on. All I wanted to do was escape and try to stop the burning.

However, before we could leave the tent, the Drill Sergeant had to see you don that mask.

Well, eventually you'd get it together, focus, concentrate, and get that mask on. Getting out of the tent wasn't the greatest reward, however, because the air aggravated the burning. You needed air, you needed water, you needed relief and you had to throw up.

This is the kind of experience you would hope to forget and never have again. God's word tells us that all things work together for them who love the Lord. Somehow, this previous gas chamber-like experience became vitally important in Belize.

During our outreach, we visited the prison in Belize. We were able to meet with the Warden and gain access into the prison area to minister. Our team was able to speak words of encouragement to the general population of the prison over their radio PA system. One other team member and I shared scripture over the PA as the inmates went about their normal, daily routine.

As the Word went forth through the airwaves, a sense of awareness began to overtake the environment. Although at that time, we were not having direct personal contact with them, they were being touched by the Living Word. Individuals, casually seeking the source of the new voices. From a distance, we could observe their bodies releasing the tension of the usual atmosphere. So much so, the atmosphere changed within the walls of the radio tower and there was a presence of peace and joy in the room.

The women of our team were able to bring personal hygiene items and minister to the women in their area of confinement. I was asked to share and encourage the women. As I sought God in what to share, in what seemed to be, such a dire situation, it was impressed upon my spirit to just encourage them to hope in God. We knew that there was not a lot that our team could do in one visit... of our own strength.

We had experienced enough in our mission outreaches to know that God would compensate for every shortcoming that man possessed. So in our assurance in God's awesomeness, we always surrendered us in exchange for his glory. We were his willing vessels. As the team prepared to be open and available for individual requests of prayer, we ministered hope and encouraged the women.

The women freely opened their hearts to the hope offered. They shared their desires to be with their children, families, and for a new life opportunity. I asked the women to form a circle of unity and the team members began to pray for each one, as we touched and agreed. Women began to weep and release.

We prayed that God would lift their burdens and set them free. Free in their spirit, mind, and body as only God could do. That the ache in their hearts would be mended by the greater love of God. That their absent children and family would know the love each still carried in her heart for them. That in the weary and lonely nights, there would be a divine comfort. That God would provide protection and cover, keeping them from all hurt and harm. We ended our prayer with a sobering request for God to manifest the fulfillment of his purpose in each of their individual lives, their Mission Possible.

In the midst of many streaming tears, the team continued to fellowship with the women. Our team members gifted the women with the hygiene items we purchased earlier that day. This fellowship time was a wondrous blessing because our team was able to spend focused one on one time with each woman. This fostered a lacking sense of significance and importance in these women. We were able to hear a little more about each woman's personal situation and give her hope for her own journey.

I must admit, entering into the men's ward of the prison was much more intimidating than the area for the women. Not in a way that was fearful, but you could see and sense that these individuals, perhaps, not only had hard experiences prior to getting here but appeared to be having a very different experience here now, which seemed to differ for the women.

The male team members had a room where inmates that were allowed out of their cells could attend the encouragement session. The women on our team were not allowed in the room, we stood in an area just outside of the room. We provided prayer intercession during the encouragement session, while the male team members prayed for individual inmates. The inmates were encouraged and motivated. Many of the men accepted Salvation and gave their lives to Christ.

Observing the encounters individuals were having with the spirit of God showed His willingness to come into any circumstance and deliver. Even in a jail cell, His mission is still possible.

Chapter 6

Rain Forest

Chapter 6
Rain Forest

*There hath no temptation taken you but such
as is common to man; but God is faithful, who
will not suffer you to be tempted above that ye
are able; but will with the temptation also
make a way to escape, that ye may be able to
bear it.*

1 Corinthians 10:13 (King James Version)

Our team traveled into the rainforest
to minister to the locals. This meant traveling
a few miles outside the city limits and
overnight lodging for a couple of days. The
next day, we loaded up to go into the
rainforest. We traveled to a site and met
another group in the area conducting cultural
research on tribal living. They were really
deep inside the rainforest. It seemed we were

driving forever before we reached their location.

Unloading from the van was like entering into a village time capsule. The research group had reconstructed a mock village. They even shared a story with our team about a watch dog who was left to guard the site during the night. When the dog went missing the next day, they presumed it had been killed by the Bobcats in the area. I couldn't tell if that really happened or not, but I didn't need much convincing. I think they sensed some of the ladies' curious awe of the rainforest; so that story was especially for us. It worked! That story reminded us to respect the rainforest and reverence from afar. Overall, we enjoyed our time with our new research group friends. Their study of the culture was very informative and helpful in our interaction with the locals.

The local tribe was made up of coffee farmers who still lived in thatched roof houses. We prayed for and with their families for God to bring them increase, healing, and blessings.

After the outreach in Belize, the team had the opportunity to have reentry time. We decided to go snorkeling. The key to this story is that I don't know how to swim. I made this very clear to our team as soon as the ideas were decided. They assured me with, "We got you". I was given a life vest, fins, and snorkeling equipment. The guide took us out to waist deep water as we viewed the coral reef. After a few minutes, we traveled further out to depths where we needed our life jackets to help us float. I had forgotten all about not being able to swim. I became so intrigued by a whole new world under the sea. Magnificently colored fish and plants I had never seen before.

After some time, we got back on the boat and traveled out for about thirty minutes. As we ventured further out into deeper waters, I quickly remembered that I can't swim. The boat stopped and we were informed that we all had to evacuate boat because all the guides were going into the water. I flipped backward off of the boat. As soon as I entered the water,

I was reminded, again that I can't swim. As we moved away from the boat, I realized the water was about thirty feet deep. I floated, kicked, and splashed with little assistance, following the guide. Everything appeared to be going great. The guide periodically pointed out interesting sites beneath us.

At one point, we swam upon an eel. It appeared to be coming in my direction. The entire group scattered. It startled me and I screamed. Yes, I SCREAMED under water! The scream's broad air bubbles broke the seal on my snorkeling gear and water began to funnel in. I thought I was going to die. I had to do something quick! Just before I slipped into full panic mode, I remembered that sealing the snorkeling equipment required the same technic as donning a gas mask. That recall may have saved my life that day.

We returned to the boat and continued on to the next location where we visited a school of stingrays. No one ever even knew about my near-death experience. Needless to say, I didn't get off the boat at the next location. On top of that, the guide had just told us a story about how stingrays killed a trainer a few days earlier. No, no, I'm good. God has provided a way of escape from my last experience. I'm not getting off this boat again until we are back on shore.

That experience reminded me that God has already equipped us for any challenge we may encounter. Remember, whatever your purpose may be, God has already equipped you for it. There will be many experiences and situations you go through that make no sense or don't seem to fit in your purpose, at all. But, don't fret, all things work together for the good of those that love the Lord and are called to His purpose.

Chapter 7

The Longest Walk In the Dominican Republic

Chapter 7
The Longest Walk In the Dominican Republic

Ask thee a sign of the Lord thy God ask it either in depth, or in the height above.

Isaiah 7:11 (King James Version)

On my first mission outreach to the Dominican Republic, I learned that you never know what could be going on around you. You should always be very attentive and aware of your surroundings. Although we were here to talk to local partners about clean water projects, there was a need brought to our attention.

One of the partners shared a story about his ongoing effort to help individuals located in a particular community. He accounted that the poverty is so great there that even after providing medical care for those infected by the contaminated water they ended up sick again because they returned to their community and consumed that same water. He had started an initiative to reach one individual per family, and give them an opportunity to leave the community, develop a skill, and help their family members back home. He asked if we would like to see this impoverished community.

To our amazement, we had been walking around, perhaps even on top of, this community every day. He led us through the city, to an area with a community located on the hillside of the elevated city. We descended below the city on, what seemed to be, steps that didn't end. We walked deeper into darkening trees until the sky almost disappeared. It seemed, the further we descended down those never ending steps, the more intense the smell and distress of the area became. Shanty houses rigged electrical wiring, dirt floors, and all of the horrific signs of poverty. As we entered the hidden community, we could see individuals sitting in the shanty homes, some almost appearing to be lurking in the darkness of the trees, and others checking us closely.

We reached the end of the seemingly never-ending steps at the edge of a river of water. It was the community's water supply. Although the water was contaminated, we saw children playing on the edge of the riverbank. We saw families washing and others using it for the bathroom.

Overwhelmed by this moment, I looked back up the hill and, without a doubt; I know God left an everlasting impression on my spirit. My question, "God how can a difference be made in such distressed and difficult places?" His response to me was, "It's not things that make a life rich and prosperous, but knowing Jesus Christ as Lord and Savior." My soul wept for those people. I was reaffirmed that I am called to a difficult work in the Kingdom of God.

Tip from the

Author:

Discipline is a tool

necessary for

achievement. Both,

personal discipline and

organizational

discipline will fuel long

sustaining

accomplishments.

Therefore, if you are

not ready for focus and

determination, your

probability for success

is low. Now is the time

to do that inventory

check and get your

priorities in order.

Standing at the bottom of that hill, wearily anticipating the climb back up to the top, I reflected on the insurmountable struggle ahead for the people living below this elevated city. As we ascended the stairs to the top of the hill, I could correlate the strain of the climb to the struggle of the individuals and families trying to improve their life circumstance and get out of the environment of this community.

That walk up those steps was the longest walk for me in the whole Dominican Republic. My legs ached, I was tired and thirsty, but still, this discomfort did not compare to the magnitude of the daily struggle for those stuck in the oppression of this community. Halfway back up the hill, several team members had to stop and make necessary adjustments to be able to continue the climb. Just like those stuck living at the bottom of this hill, sustaining themselves with the contaminated water, I thought, they, too, may have to stop and make the necessary adjustment to be able to continue the task of changing their environment.

At the top of this "mountain" hill, I realized that the purpose in my life will continue because of the hardships that many people are experiencing in this world. Regardless of how difficult or trying, my mission is possible.

Because of what God has done in my life, I

have been given the opportunity to make a

difference in the lives of others.

Chapter 8

Bears In A Tree In Cambodia

Chapter 8
Bears In A Tree In Cambodia

*Just look at your own calling, believers, not
many (of you were considered) wise
according to human standards, not many
powerful or influential, not many of high and
noble birth. But God has selected (for his
Purpose) the foolish things of the world to
shame the wise (revealing their ignorance),
and God has selected (for his Purpose) the
weak things of the world to shame the thing
which is strong (revealing their frailty).*

1 Corinthians 1:26-27 (AMP)

Our team traveled to Cambodia to
work with women and children who had
escaped the human trafficking industry. This
was our second year. The focus this year was
exhorting staff of this organization, as well as,
helping the women. During our time there, a
sweet presence of peace settled in the room.

The ladies, both staff, and ex-trafficking victims wept in the presence. Internal burdens that weighed them down had been lifted.

The next day's assignment was to work with the children delivered from human trafficking. We were so excited. Because we were there in December, we were able to have a Christmas theme for our party activities. We planned all kinds of fun activities that included a pizza party and gifts for each child. Little did we know, the children had a surprise waiting for us, too.

Everyone was excited to plan, shop, and organize whatever needed to ensure that the children felt the presence of love. Team members volunteered to dress as clowns, paint faces, play board games, etc. We decorated the grounds of the compound with colorful balloons and set up several play stations for face painting, bowling, jump rope, bible trivia, etc. Playful streamers were hanging from trees. The surprise gift of a doll for every little girl.

The party began with clowns playing and dancing with the children. The children giggled, played, and ran from station to station. The team members participated fully, jumping and running as if they had regained their youth.

At the end of the day, we had our pizza party, cake and ice cream, with the surprise gift of a doll for each little girl. As we started the party, you could see the girls' eyes enlarge with enthusiasm. They had planned to sing songs for us. As they presented us with their songs, we presented them with their gifts. As they embraced their new best friends, each little girl slipped away to a Christmas tree which had been decorated with bears. Each girl took a bear from the tree and presented it to each team member. This small gesture brought each of us to tears. We were so excited about what we had planned for them, but they had a plan that totally caught us off guard. This is the day we saw bears in a tree in Cambodia.

Tip from the

Author:

Invite exposure into
your life, both
professionally and
personally. Don't resist
the new or the
unfamiliar. Glean from
the opportunities
exposure presents and
learn from every
experience. It's all part
of your journey.

Overwhelmed with love, I was reminded that
we can make plans but God can completely
alter them. I will no longer place limitations
on how God can bless my life. Those things

that *should* disqualify you, God uses to help

fulfill His purpose in your life.

Chapter 9

Standing in the Nations

Chapter 9
Standing in the Nations

*Hear instruction, and be wise, and refuse it
not.*

Proverbs 8:33 (King James Version)

In all of these experiences, I never
would have dreamed it was possible for me. I
just started moving one day and found myself
standing in the nations.

When God first provided the opportunity for
me to bloom in my purpose, I could only
perceive going on a trip. Over time, I began to
view the work and interaction with the
various people as an extension of God's love,
unaware of how the effects of that love would

saturate every area of my life. My priorities were completely refocused. Even my family joked about how little I stayed in the US. When I did get to spend time with family at holidays or gatherings, they would ask about my experiences. This was a set up to share the gospel with my family.

I often spoke with family about God's goodness, love, power, and the amazing ability I had to experience it all. As they saw me change, they wanted to know more about what was changing me. I got to tell them about my Jesus!

I started out, on what I thought, were trips, but turned out to be divine missions that were significant to my purpose. One day, the revelation hit me that sometimes you could be living your purpose and dying to be somewhere else. It was in that moment that I rearranged my life for this opportunity and determined that everything in my world had to submit to my purpose.

Believe me; I had to weather a lot of storms just to stand. I was challenged in every area of my life. But I learned that God is not limited to my experiences, He is much bigger. Is there anything too hard for your God?

Chapter 10

Pre-Destined

Chapter 10
Pre-destined

Before I formed you in the womb I knew you,
before you were born I set you apart; I
appointed you as a prophet to the nations.

Jeremiah 1:5 (NIV)

Jeremiah's name means *healed by and*
supported of Yah (God). He is the son of
Anathoth, a priest. He was called, by God to
be a prophet, throughout the reign of three
other kings of Judah; Josiah, Jehoiakim, and
Zedekiah. No one believed Jeremiah's
prophecies and during Jeremiah's time as a
prophet, the people of Jerusalem went into
exile in Babylon. Josiah instituted major
religious change, reforms in temple worship,
and established or compiled important

Hebrew Scriptures. He became King at the age of eight, after the assassination of his father, King Amon. Josiah reigned for 31 years. He was very righteous, walked in the way of David, and turned not aside to the right hand or to the left (2 Kings 22:2). He encouraged exclusive worship to Yahweh, forbidding all other forms of worship, reinstituted the Passover celebration, and returned the Ark of the Covenant.

Jehoiakim's name means, whom Jehovah sets up, or Yahweh will establish. Jehoiakim reigned as king, for 11 years, on the principals of luxury, extortion, and idolatry. Three years into his reign, Nebuchadnezzar, the oppressor, carried part of his princes and treasures to Babylon. He, too, ignored the warnings of Jeremiah.

He was taken captive by Nebuchadnezzar, along with Daniel (Belteshazzar) and three companions Shadrach, Meshach, and Abed-nego. Jehoiakim was killed and his body was thrown over the wall of Jerusalem. He was drug away and unburied, meaning he was not given the honor of burial. His sin of abomination became known as a desecration of the sanctuary.

Jehoiakim saw a miraculous deliverance for Jerusalem. Because of this, Jehoiakim and the people believed that Jerusalem would always stand. Jeremiah, however, saw their lives were not pleasing to God and had to change.

Therefore, Jeremiah believed the captivity would cleanse Jerusalem. So when Jeremiah prophesied the captivity, King Jehoiakim and the people would not believe. Jeremiah had to stand-alone on his prophecy.

Zedekiah was the last King of Judah, before the exile and destruction of Babylon. During his reign, false prophets and diviners arose to spread lies about the captivity. But, Jeremiah reminded the people that the exile would last its duration because it was from God. They were being punished because they had turned from God and the Torah.

Jeremiah admonished them to build houses, dwell in their land of captivity, plant gardens, eat their fruit, take wives, bring up children,

take wives for their sons, give daughters in
marriage, multiply and not be diminished.
Pray for the welfare of the city, for their own
good. Jeremiah also continued to warn
Jerusalem to repent.

Jeremiah was accused of being an agent of
the enemy and was thrown in jail. Jeremiah
was thrown into mud pits and almost
drowned. Nebuchadnezzar captured
Jerusalem and invited Jeremiah to come to
Babylon as an honored guest. He declined
and remained in Jerusalem. That is where
Jeremiah spent his last days, in Judah.

This captivity ended the kingdom of David
until it shall be restored again. But God
promised, "Yet, for all that, though they may

be in the land of their enemies; will I not cast them away, neither will I despise them to destroy them completely, to break my covenant with them. And I will remember unto them the covenant of their ancestors, whom I brought forth out of the land of Egypt before the eyes of the nations that I may be unto them, God." (Lev. 26:44-45)

Like Jeremiah, you and I may find ourselves in our response to God's assignment for us, experiencing many varying seasons. Times when everything in the world is working for us, and times when everything is working against us. We may find ourselves standing alone on the word God has given to us. No one confirming, agreeing or believing in what

God is doing in your life. But, we will have to remember who formed us and created us with a purpose in mind.

He sanctified us and made us significant requiring respect. He ordained us, gives us approval, sealed us, and he is backing us. Our mission is not one that we determine, but it has been established by God. Therefore, as we move into action, opening our hearts and minds to receive God opportunities, go with the assurance that He will lead you into your purpose and make your mission possible.

We may be concerned about God's assignment for our lives. We may feel it is too great for us. That we are too young or too old. Or, that we don't have the knowledge or experience. But, with God's support, we don't have to be concerned. God will give us what we need when we need it. God has touched us and put his word in our hearts.

Sometimes, the assignment you have could be just as difficult as Jeremiah's.
You may have to stand alone. You may even be rejected. But we must not be afraid, for God is always with us and the assigned purpose He has ordained you for was predetermined for you with an expected end. He shall finish the work he has started in you and you shall see the manifestation of what God has spoken about your life.

Chapter 11

The Call

Chapter 11
The Call

For the gifts and the calling of God are irrevocable for he does not withdraw what he has given, nor does he change his mind about those to whom he gives his grace or to whom he sends his call.

Romans 11:29 (AMP)

There is an assurance in the "Call" of God. When He endows you with a purpose, it is impossible to revoke and incapable of being changed. Even God says he will not take back his Word or remove his call.

When I reflect on my relationship with the Lord, I must admit there have been many times when I have been reluctant to respond. I didn't have the capacity to see what God knew about me. I intellectually comprehended the words he spoke about my life, but I could not visualize them in my life and experiences. I spent so much time questioning or, negotiating the purpose that eventually there was no choice but to do.

Tip from the

Author:

Involve yourself with

people and things of

God. Isolation is a tactic

of the enemy. When

you are always a loner,

your thoughts dominate

your time. In positive

company, you absorb

positivity. Also, being

people-oriented creates

a necessary link

between you and others.

We all need someone,

and someone needs you

to fulfill our purpose.

Although difficult, I found that even my smallest efforts to accept and move toward my purpose were significant. My movement created a point of contact for God to touch my life. With each effort, God led me to the next step toward the purpose he created for my life. With each step, I discovered more about myself that I didn't know about, gifts God had hidden within me.

As you are moving forward in the purpose of God for your life, you may not even recognize the progression being made through your small efforts. Remaining steadfast will allow you to experience standing in purpose. So don't waste time concerning yourself with things God already justified and will use to qualify you for his purpose.

Chapter 12

The World Awaits

Chapter 12
The World Awaits

*For we know that the whole creation has been
moaning together as in the pains of childbirth
until now. And not only this, but we too, who
have the first fruit of the Spirit (a joyful
indication of the blessings to come), even we
groan inwardly, as we wait eagerly for (the
sign
of) our adoption as sons – the redemption and
transformation of our body (at the
resurrection).*
Romans 8:22-23 (APB)

I've shared my stories with you to
encourage you to move into creating
remarkable stories in your life through your
experiences. God is no respecter of persons,
as he moved me into my purpose, he will do
the same for you! Throughout my years of
training and leading mission teams into many
countries, I found my *Mission Possible*

purpose already occurring in my life. Because of my experiences, I can boldly affirm that "All Things Are Possible" with God.

Sometimes we hold ourselves back or remain in that stagnant, unfulfilling place in our lives. Overtime, we begin to believe that we may have nothing to offer, at all; because who knows you better than you, right? The reality is, God knows you better than you know yourself. He created and custom built you for a divine purpose, a mission that He wants to make possible in you. Our gifts from God are tied together within his plans for the body of Christ; the church. Everyone brings something to the table that is beneficial for the whole. In Ephesians 4:16, God tells us that we are fitly joined together, necessary for the supply of one another. It's God's perfect plan, where each and every one of us are strategically joined, knitted firmly together by what each person individual purpose. When each part is working properly, the 'church body' grows and matures, building itself up in (unselfish) love.

There are some hidden treasures of gifts and talents that have been embedded in you. As you are exposed to different experiences and opportunities, those hidden gems will become activated. Because we spend most of our life living our natural experiences, we are mentally limited. There are past experiences that you presently saw no use, but even those will be useful for you to continue your movement in God's' purpose for your life. We must recognize that as we grow in our spiritual relationship with God there are always new revelations, experiences, and situations tailor fit to help us continue to take steps in our purpose.

I admonish you to move freely and liberally into experiencing Gods spiritual promises he has spoken over your life. There will always be obstacles, but remember, everything you need to overcome them is already inside you. You must tap into your God given purpose.

The work that God is doing in you is not just for you. As a member of the greater body of Christ you have a responsibility to be concerned for the good of others. We should look out into the world and see God opportunities all around us. There are numerous ways in which God could use you to show forth his glory in this world. If we were to take an assessment of our lives, we could find a "Christmas at the Dump" kind of moment. The type of moment where the hurt and pain of others approaches you and stares you right in the face. Being faced with insurmountable poverty and despair, we are forced to be grateful for every blessing. Recognizing that small things matter could be the catalyst to bring you into a "Shoes flying in Africa" kind of experience. Where you are the resource God uses to be a blessing in someone else's life, meeting a personal need that someone had waited and prayed about for a long time. When you are willing to move into opportunities that may not seem to have a huge impact, it could very well be the opportunity that brings about the miracle. Jesus' first miracle was not performed on a grand stage and wasn't even scheduled, but opportunity presented itself. What opportunities are awaiting you? Move and find out!

There are times when we are existing but not living at all, disconnected from the world and environments around us. We should ask God to open our spiritual eyes so that we may see this world as He sees it. Are we standing next to our miracle unaware?

We should not discount any of our experiences. They are all apart of God's guidance, directing us into our purpose. We know, according to His word all things work together for our good. Then, we should fully embrace the good and the bad. It is not easy having total reliance and trust in God, but I have found that it is the only sure way for me to reach my full potential in this life. When our team entered the rainforest in Belize, it was somewhat intimidating and frightening. I've found that sometimes the things that God reveals to us can cause us to have a similar kind of response. After my many years of performing outreach missions, I've found that complete obedience helps eliminate most of

those feelings. I, then, rest in the assurance
that God sent me and he has me covered. The
enemy cannot contain you when you're in
God's will, he can only try to distract you but
God has already made your way of escape.
As we walked around in the Dominican
Republic, we found another group of people
in great need. We were able to bless and
change lives there, simply because we were
willing to deviate from our set agenda and let
God lead. More personally, if we had not
allowed for this momentary detour, I would
not have had my moment of revelation in
which God assured me that my call might be
hard, but it was going to be rewarding. It is in
odd moments like this that God has spoken
destiny to me. In Mexico, "you are supposed

to be here". On the plane to Africa, "you were born for such a time as this". What I learned is that you can never determine where, when, or how God will manifest in your life. Your responsibilities are to be alert and to move when he speaks. This is a military-like concept I've adopted in my spiritual walk with God. You must continue to push even when it is difficult and challenging.

You find little blessings from the Lord throughout your life journey with him. In Cambodia, it was something as simple as bears in a tree. Oh how it softened my heart to receive such an unexpected gift from the children whose lives had been entangled in human trafficking. Just another example of how, in the midst of the most trying of times of life, the smallest gesture of kindness has impact. The little things you do make a tremendous difference in the lives of others. Don't put limitations on how God can use you to be a blessing in others' lives. If you are willing to follow God's' instruction, He will guide you into your predestined purpose.

The Bible tells us to not despise small beginnings. Your journey may start out looking like one thing and somewhere along the path there is a shift or change that occurs. But as you continue the journey; it metamorphoses into something greater than you could have imagined. This is because Gods' thoughts and plans for us are much higher than our own and always will be. So, I encourage you to think higher, without limits

and move toward his plans for you.

If You Move, God Moves

Interactive motivation to help you move
toward your *Mission Possible*

And we know (with great confidence) that God (who is deeply concerned about us) causes all things to work together (as a plan) for good for those who love God, to those who are called according to His plan and purpose. **Romans 8:28 (ABV)**

It is time for you to start taking your small steps into your destiny. Small steps of continuous improvement in what God has purposed for your life. So, if you are worried that your first step will be unwarranted, the application of the Kaizen philosophy will cover your efforts. This way of thinking, in its origin, inspires you to move with the acknowledgement that you will have to continuously improve your efforts. Inconsistencies won't hinder or derail you if you just continue. You must move first before

God begins to work on your behalf.

How can you apply the Kaizen philosophy to moving toward the mission God has purposed for you?

Trust in the Lord with all thine heart; and lean not unto thine own understanding.
Proverbs 3:5 (KJV)

Proverbs is a book of wisdom, exhortation and instruction. This particular verse emphasizes that trust in God requires all of your heart and usually manifests itself in ways you won't understand. We should purpose in our hearts to rely solely upon God and not on our own resources, information, plans, and self-confidence. We should plan to be led by the Lord. Then and only then will you begin to experience the peace of walking in your purpose.

What are some things stopping you from trusting God, wholeheartedly, with your life's purpose?

For I know the thoughts that I think toward you, saith the Lord, thoughts of peace, and not of evil, to give you an expected end.
Jeremiah 29:11 (KJV)

This scripture is the prophecy of the Prophet Jeremiah to the captives in Babylon, which he sent via letters. He was advising them, while in captivity, that God still had them on his mind; God's thoughts toward them were good, filled with love.

Although, their circumstance (captivity) did not look very promising, God's original plan for their lives had not changed. We may feel like we are being held captive by our current life situations, but God already knows how our story is going to end. He is orchestrating even the smallest moments that propel us to

our destiny; making our *Mission Possible*.

God will reveal your purpose to you, in many ways. A prophecy, direct communication, signs, etc. What are some things that God has already revealed to you about your purpose?

And those whom He predestined, He also called; and those whom He called, He also justified (declared free of the guilt of sin); and those whom He justified, He also glorified (raising them to a heavenly dignity). **Romans 8:30 (APV)**

Another reminder that God has, from the beginning, determined our life's outcome in Him. In the Bible, when God spoke resoundingly, it was to establish. Believe within your heart that God has established a unique mission within you that only you can accomplish. He has stamped his seal of approval upon it and secured it in the heavens. You are free and have access to all powers of Heaven.

Hint: your mission usually has something to do with your God-given gifts and talents. Trying to find your purpose in God? Start there. What are some gifts or talents God has established in you?

He made known to us the mystery of His will according to His good pleasure, which He purposes in Christ, with regard to the fulfillment of the times to bring all things together in Christ, things in heaven and things on the earth. **Ephesians 1:9-10 (KJV)**

We may not get all the answers we think we deserve in life, but this verse assures us that God has revealed some things to us. Things about our purpose and our mission in this life.

During my outreach missions, I realized that I was already living the promise that God had spoken to me years ago. Traveling amongst nations, cultures, and desperate people, I had only focused on the interesting moments as a 'memorable experience'. But, those steps I took across foreign lands were so much more than that. In retrospect, I concluded that God had revealed this epiphany to me many times before. Through His words to me, special interactions with others, and multiple other signs. I just missed it, too enthralled in my own feelings and plans.

What I learned? Always keep a listening ear and a keen eye open to what God is doing in you. You, like me, could be overlooking the turning point you've been praying and working for.

Take a moment to assess your life now. Are you living in your purpose, unaware? What does walking in your purpose "look like" to you?

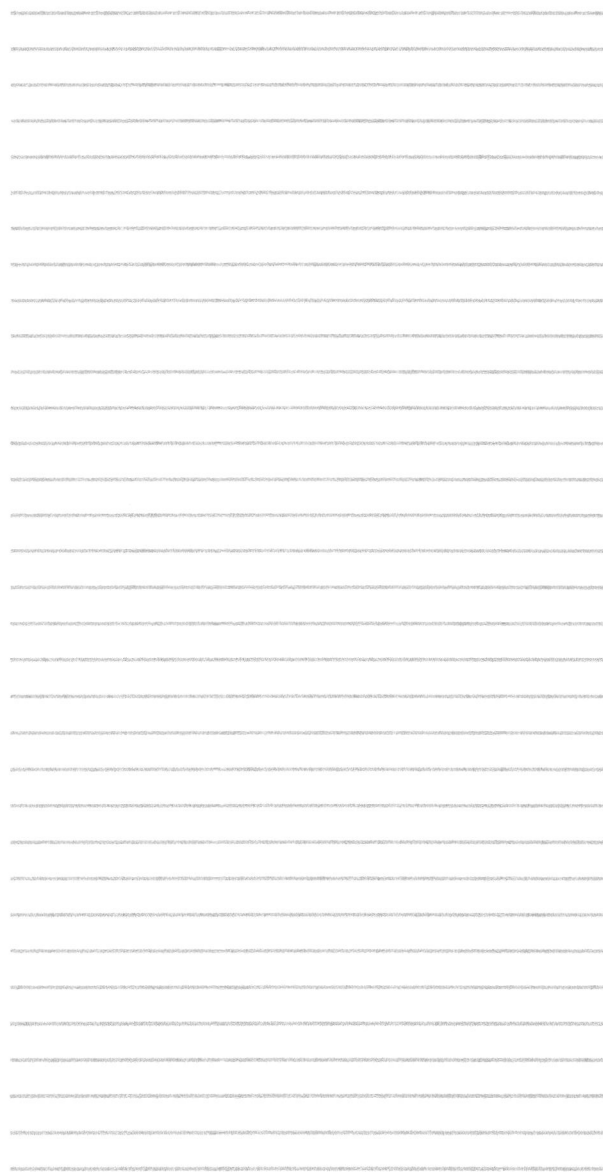

What then shall we say to all these things? If God is for us, who can be (successful) against us? **Romans 8:31 (APV)**

Here's a tip: God doesn't ask questions He doesn't already have the answer for. Instead, the perspective should read something like, "How could we not trust him?" We come to believe by hearing, but trust requires that we come into a place of complete reliance upon God.

Know that when you take your first step, whether small or large, there may be challenges. See these challenges or rough times as opportunities to honestly investigate and improve your next forward steps toward your mission. Assessing will bring about a new level of knowledge and self-confidence

in your mission walk. Know that, regardless

of what your circumstances look like, who

supports you, or even how you feel, your

purpose is still alive, divine, and possible.

The bottom line is; If you move for God, God

will move for you.

What are some small steps you can start taking today, toward your mission, to encourage God's movement in your life?

Closing Remarks

My prayer is that reading this book has caused you to really consider your next steps toward God's' plan for your life. That the stories shared, encouraged you to seize opportunities with a new outlook. Trust that every small step you take moves you closer in experiencing what God has in store for you. Set aside time to complete the *When You Move, Then God Moves,* interactive motivation questions after this chapter to help determine how to take the next steps toward your *Mission Possible*.

For (even the whole) creation (all nature)
waits eagerly for the children of God to be
revealed. **Romans 8:19 (APB)**

As you begin to move into the things of God, be confident in His divine plans for you. All of creation awaits you.

Stay tuned for the second edition of Mission Possible, The World Awaits, where you will be introduced to the vast benefits of moving in God's will. Discover how your individual purpose impacts the entire world and everything in it.